The Gifts that Lie Hidden within Difficult Emotions

Part 3: Feeling Lack and Not Enough

Yuichi Handa, PhD

Book Layout ©2017 BookDesignTemplates.com
Cover Design by Islam Farid
Editing by Kim Derby

The Gifts that Lie Hidden within Difficult Emotions (Part 3): Feeling Lack and Not Enough/ Yuichi Handa. -- 1st ed.
Printed in the United States of America
ISBN 13: 978-1976052750

Table of Contents

Dedication

I offer my deepest appreciation to the wonderful people I met during my recent travels in Bali, many of whom practice a generosity of spirit that inspires me daily.

1 Preface

Hello, dear reader! Thank you for your purchase of this little book.

If this is the first book in the series you're reading, welcome, and I hope you find something of value in here. Although this current book can work as a stand-alone guide to the topic, it may help to read the first book in the series for a clearer and more elaborate comprehension of some of the processes I refer to in this book.

Also, this book is meant to be read more than once. During your first read, you may glean and gather information along the way, but it's likely during your second or third readings that your understanding of the collection of ideas and practices will come together as a whole.

And for those of you who have already read through either the first, second, or both books in the series, welcome back and thank you for your continued readership! Although it may not turn out to be the case for you, this book may draw more resistance from you than the previous two. There is a very particular reason for this, which is that this book more than any of the others, targets the ego. Specifically, it addresses pride, a natural source of resistance. My hope is that you will consider the ideas here, and even vet it against your own experience as well as what you observe in those around you, and if you notice any level of resonance, that you allow in the ideas and practices into your daily life and being. I speak from my own personal experience when I say that the ideas in this particular volume can help transform one's life in ways that may seem unimaginable prior to the transformation, until they begin to show and materialize in one's life.

Lastly, if you have yet to download the free companion guide to part one, which is a short 20-page-ish guide on working with anxiety and constriction around the heart (titled *What Lies Beneath Your Dread and Anxiety and How to Relax within It*), please go to www.yuichihanda.com/signup. Signing up there will also have the additional effect of putting you on the notifications list for my future publications, in case that is or becomes of interest to you!

2 Introduction: Not enough

Welcome to the third installment of the series. This book is about lack. It's about feeling as if one doesn't have enough. Or simply, one *isn't* enough.

Maybe this shows up for you in regards to your finances and material possessions. Or with your time. You never feel that you have enough. Your mind is regularly focused on what more you could have—materially, financially, or temporally—that would make things better. Fuller.

Or maybe it shows up in your social relationships, such as in feeling that you don't have enough friends or love in your life. Or if you do have friends, maybe there's a sense that more would be better. Or that you need a partner, and if you already have one, that you need another partner. This is still a sense of lack.

Maybe it goes even deeper, and you suffer from a chronic and/or underlying feeling as if you yourself aren't enough, as if there's a profound deficiency in you that you just can't seem to get over. "Something must be wrong with me" has become your secret mantra. And because this sense of inner lack is always sitting right beneath the surface, maybe you take slights from others easily, as if every semi-critical comment were a confirmation of your self-assessment of internal lack.

Or maybe it shows up simply as low-grade yet chronic insecurity that's easily triggered by various life circumstances.

It doesn't matter how it shows up. If it shows up for you in one area, it'll likely show up in other areas. It may not be so obvious in how it shows up elsewhere, but if you look carefully, you'll likely find the same feeling of lack lurking beneath the surface.

This will be the topic of exploration.

3 The solution

It's really very simple.

The solution to not feeling enough is to give, to act generously, to offer something of value and substance. That's all there is to it.

Let's take the case of material feelings of lack.

Apparently, some folks have made the long and arduous trek to Dharamsala, India and waited for days to gain an audience with the Dalai Lama just to ask him this one question of, "How do I become rich?"

From what I've read, his response is a good hearty laugh and then the response of, "Give away everything you have!"

The same idea shows up in the Christian practice of tithing. If you want to experience abundance, cultivate the habit of giving.

Similarly, if you feel that you're lacking in friends, then be a good friend to others. Those who feel rich in relationships understand this on some level of their being. And if you observe people who are lacking (or *feeling* that they lack) in friendships, that's the first thing you might notice; they're not focused on being a great friend *to* others. Many times they're more focused on themselves and what they can get *from* others. They could use people, sometimes subtly, sometimes obviously—that is, they use people for their own fulfillment or escape, such as to assuage their own loneliness or unhappiness, to bolster their self-esteem, to further their agenda, and so on.

And if you feel lacking within, then give yourself fully and freely to life in all its aspects. It's rare to find someone who's *deeply* involved with the world around them in a capacity of *genuine* giving who feels lacking at their core.

So again, it's simple. To overcome lack, give.

But simple doesn't mean easy. Or even straightforward, since giving away crap isn't the same as giving something of value and substance. And when we feel lacking, we often don't consider what we have to offer as being of value.

But also, when we feel lacking, we sometimes give with expectations, which amounts to not truly giving.

Simply stated, it's not so easy to go from poverty-mentality to uber-generosity. If you're one of those rare people who can, then good for you. You don't need this book. But if you aren't, then I hope something here will spark an interest in you, enough to move you from not enough to enough and possibly even to plenty.

4 Repetition

So where do we start?

We start by identifying the sense of lack that we carry within ourselves. (Maybe we jot down on a piece of paper where we experience this sense of not having or being enough so that it's directly in front of us. If you're an artist, maybe you can sketch an image that captures this feeling for you. It can help to have something in front of you, to have some representation or expression of the sense of lack.)

And this becomes our regular meal. That is, we take it in. We stop running from it, and instead, we invite it into our awareness and learn to sit with it. In this way, we ingest it, digest it, and process it again and again. We try our best not to deviate from it. We explore the feeling with as much curiosity as we're able to muster.

This is what we do.

If you skip this step and assume that reading this book and just *thinking* about things will solve your problem, you might consider going back and reading book one. It doesn't work just to *think* things through.

You have to work away at the *feeling and experience* of not enough. You're not conquering it. You're succumbing to it. That is, you're leaning into it, giving yourself over to it. You're processing and digesting it. You're sitting with it and letting it course through your veins, your entire being. And you're trusting that your organism will know how to extract out the nutrients contained within this God-awful feeling of lack as you allow for it to be within you. It's these nutrients you're after. And you only obtain them from digesting the feeling.

(If the idea of sussing out your feelings of lack seems a bit abstract or subtle, then a more action-oriented way to go about it is to find a hobby where you regularly feel lacking or less than. Pursue that, and you'll have plenty on your plate!)

So that's all you need do. That will get you from lack to generosity to plenty.

The rest of this book will simply highlight the journey. It'll illustrate the signposts you can expect to pass along your journey of "eating"—that is, taking in, digesting, and releasing (pooping)—your feelings of insufficiency and lack.

5 Fishing expedition

What if you don't find yourself feeling particularly generous, and at the same time, you don't relate to this sense of lack or not enough?

It could be that you're just fine.

Or it could be that you haven't looked very carefully.

If it's the former, maybe this book isn't for you? But just in case the latter is closer to the truth, we'll go on a brief excursion for the next few sections to see if less obvious features of lack aren't cropping up in your life and in your psyche.

6 Defensiveness as a symptom of lack

What happens when we feel that we're not enough? A common tendency is to easily become defensive. We *perceive* even the most benign input as a slight or put down, and we *perceive* out-right criticism as violence. But that's not how it has to be.

For someone who doesn't have this problem but instead has a more "abundant" attitude, a critical remark can be a welcome bit of input toward improvement, whether of a facet of life or of oneself. This is how much of science progresses, for example—through tough criticism from peers and colleagues.

But when there's an underlying feeling or belief of lack, it's hard to take this attitude. Think of an area of your life where you feel lacking, where you feel "not enough." How do you react internally to criticism or even mild non-support? You likely close down in some way, right?

This is what I'm calling defensiveness.

When I was younger and I would play music, it didn't matter what anyone said to me. I "knew" that they were just being nice and that I had no talent. It didn't matter that my music brought delight to some. It didn't even matter that they said nice things about my playing. I couldn't hear the praise. And God forbid if they said anything mildly constructive. It would be all I needed to convince myself that I shouldn't even be trying. So I'd shut down. Stop playing for weeks, even months.

It's silly now, kind of childish and immature when I think about it. But it was real to me. I wasn't trying to be that way. I was just very sensitive in that area.

But what undergirded my over-sensitivity was that I felt that I simply wasn't good enough as a musician, and I couldn't shake that belief. Sadly, it became a self-fulfilling prophecy. Because I wasn't open to input, my improvement was slow or mostly non-existent, which was in dramatic contrast to other areas of my life where I wasn't so sensitive to input.

So if you're having any trouble finding where you might have a sense of lack, just look where you tend to be sensitive, defensive, or even shut down. You'll likely find that underlying feeling of not being good enough there.

7 Closed-minded

If you've ever been accused of being closed-minded, this could be a hint of defensiveness in you, of shutting down to input. It may not be, but it could. If you hear such a comment coming your way, think of it as the universe telling you that there may be a sense of lack underneath.

Try to receive such a comment as a gift, pointing your attention to something that may be calling to you.

If you look carefully enough—unless it's already patently clear to you—you may find a pervasive sense of something not being enough, whether of yourself or of some facet of yourself (as you may have neatly compartmentalized it in your mind).

8 More

When there's a sense of lack, there's a tendency then to want more.

Maybe you've become a hoarder. Or maybe you call it "collecting," as in "I'm a collector of fine things." It's the same thing. It's usually a compensation for an underlying lack.

Collecting can look like you're collecting coins or fine wine. Or it can look like you're obsessed with having *more* money. Or it can show up in human relationships, such as wanting *more* friends, or maybe more and more partners. You just want *more.* Maybe it's *more* experiences. That's still the same thing.

It's fashionable nowadays to say, "I don't need more *things*, but I'm all about experiencing more that life has to offer." That sounds nice, like you're not materialistic but you're just transferring the same materialistic attitude toward your experiences. It's still a form of hoarding. You could probably become a popular blogger by saying these kinds of things (because you'd then be co-signing the rampant expansionism of your readers). But that doesn't change the underlying dynamic. You're still encouraging stockpiling something called "experiences," or seen from another perspective, hoarding more memories. It doesn't change the fact that you still may be operating from an underlying sense of lack, of your past and current experiences simply not being enough.

But they are. That's the fact of the matter. You don't need to collect 1000 *new* experiences to be full. Having the same deeply connecting and meaningful experience on a regular basis, *especially if it continues to deepen* as in a meditation practice or an intimate relationship, can be enough.

It's subtle. It's easy to buy into the need for more in this culture (or whatever culture you happen to be in). It can take on a "healthy" hue, as if you're not really living unless you're checking off your bucket list. But it can still be the same cover-up for not enough.[1]

---

[1] This in no way is a rant against exploration, expansion, travel, meeting new people, and the like. I simply am pointing to the underlying dynamic in some of these pursuits. You can know whether the urge for expansion and travel, say, is based upon lack or a more intrinsic interest. Simply examine how it feels when you're *not* doing it. If something feels missing, then there's the lack. Plain and simple. But if you are just as content and fulfilled when not engaging in these activities, then what lack is there to speak of?

9 Addiction

If the sense of deprivation is acute, you might take it further and become an addict, whether to drugs and alcohol, work, shopping, gambling, co-dependent relationships, sex, television, the internet, Facebook and Twitter, video games, extreme exercise, travel, escape, to anything—it doesn't matter. It's all to fill a hole, a lack within.

It's what Buddhists call the "hungry ghost," an apparition with a bottomless stomach symbolizing this eternal hunger and emptiness inside that nothing can ever fill. That's the image of addiction.

10 Procrastination and the fear of failure

Maybe you occasionally suffer from a fear of failure? You might look into that as well.

If you ask yourself, "What's so bad about failing," you might find it's not the actual failing which is the problem, but what it says about *you* that's the real issue at hand.

And what does it say about you? It doesn't say anything, but if you suffer from this fear, it might say for you that you're not enough. You're not good enough.

And maybe you don't want to be confronted with this seeming truth, so you decide not to try. You never even begin.

11 Pride

So what do we call it when we're defensive, closed-minded, and fearful of failure?

It's nothing other than pride.

Pride is "I know best," which is a cover-up for "I don't want to be found out that I really don't, and that I'm really not good enough deep inside."

At its root, pride isn't about a comparison with others, as in "I'm better than you," although that's how others might take it. It's really about an interior struggle within oneself. It's an attempt to keep the "not good enough" feeling at bay. So, anything that triggers it, we keep away. This results in the closed-mindedness and defensiveness. We'll do anything to keep from having to feel—no, to *know*—that we're not enough.

It can also show up as feeling like a "phony."

We might tell ourselves intellectually that we're enough. We might say affirmations or do positive thinking exercises, but somewhere deep down, we know. We know there's that part of us that feels we're not enough. And so we do everything we can to keep it at bay.

And very few around us, if anyone at all, know this truth. They just see our defensiveness. They just see our pride ("I don't need your help. I know better than you.").

But if we look carefully enough, what we'll see is a desire to protect ourselves from facing our own sense of lack, that huge gaping hole that sits within us. This is the interior landscape of pride.

12 Smallishness and resignation

And what happens then?

Our lives become smaller and smaller, simply because we don't want to be reminded.

We don't take risks that would trigger our sense of not being enough. Maybe we take risks in areas that don't matter so much. But God forbid we consider an endeavor that would risk failure where it mattered most to us. No, we'd much rather resign ourselves to not even trying.

So we live out a lukewarm existence, lacking in any real passion or depth. Because we're not willing to risk facing it. Not failure itself, but having to feel our inner lack.

So we become *resigned.*

If you recognize a feeling of resignation within you, or regarding a particular area of your life, you might look more carefully at this. What you might find underneath is the same sense of not being enough.

And why are some of us so stuck like this?

It's because we don't think to do the simplest thing imaginable that we can do with it, which is simply to allow for it to be. We don't think to say, "Hey, it's wonderful that I get to experience this very human feeling of not being enough." We don't think to embrace it as we would the experience of falling in love or happening upon the sublime. In other words, we don't take it in. We don't eat it. Instead, we consciously and unconsciously do everything in our power to avoid it. We try to reason our way against it by telling ourselves that we're enough. But this is just resistance to an arising emotion or experience. We're not allowing for what's occurring, and through that, we stay poor. Poor in spirit. Poor in heart. Poor in the way in which we approach living.

13 Richness revealed

So what happens when we learn to sit with our feeling of lack and start eating it?

We relax around it. We slowly stop fearing it. As a result, we slowly notice ourselves more open to new ideas and experiences that we may have been closed off to before. In terms of our relationships, we become more open to input from others (which means we gain access to additional points of information, adding to our sense of resourcefulness); we slowly begin expanding what comes into our lives. In turn, we may begin to seek out advice, even criticism, from others. We stop taking things personally. We can sift out other people's agendas from what they're truly offering. And we recognize that each person around us has much to offer us. This feels like richness.

Of course, I just condensed a process of many weeks, months, and possibly years into one paragraph. But that's the path. We go from "not enough" to richness and abundance. We become resourceful beyond what we imagined possible. We begin to recognize that this richness has been around us all along. We were focused on what was lacking in and about us. Not on what was actually there.

It's akin to the image of the little boy standing in a river with a cup in hand, crying to the heavens for water.

As we begin to open up to the richness around us, we recognize that we were standing in the richness of the desired waters the whole time!

This image of the little boy captures the essence of the "not enough" phenomenon. It's a little different from simply not seeing that one is standing in a river, although that's part of it too. And yet, it has more to do with the fact that the boy is *attached* to obtaining water in the form of rain. It has to do with the boy's *preference* of rainwater over river water, thus blinding him to the riches around him. ***It's this attachment to preference that undergirds poverty mentality.***

In short, it's our attachment to our likes and dislikes that motivates defensiveness, pride, closed-mindedness, smallishness of life, and so on and so forth.

We had to work with our confusion and our stuckness—from my previous two books—so that we could become open in our being and no longer fixated on looking in the wrong direction. This allows us to notice that we're standing in the richness of the waters we so long for. But that isn't enough. We also must learn to let go of our preference for rainwater when river water is what we are immersed in already.

It's this detachment from preference that is the gift of eating our lack. If we learn to sit with and digest our feelings of not-enoughness, we'll begin to move more assuredly in the direction of loosening our attachments to our preferences, which in turn begins to open us up to the richness of life itself.

14 The opposite of lack

So the opposite of not enough isn't enough or sufficiency. That's a strange thing to say, isn't it? But it's pragmatically true, meaning there's no practical value in believing it to be otherwise. Trying to convince yourself that you're enough, or that you have enough isn't going to help with your sense of lack. It's like a Band-Aid to your wounding. It'll only cover up but not heal.

If you suffer from symptoms of lack, it would also behoove you to get off the abundance and manifestation train. That's not going to do you any good either. You could do affirmations and visualizations about abundance till you're blue in the face, but doing this you'll never address the underlying issue, which has to do with attachment to your preferences. *Your version of abundance will always be prone to collapse.* You probably know people like this, or maybe you've done it yourself (just as I have). You try manifesting abundance, and it works for a while, but then, the whole thing gives way. *It won't naturally sustain itself since it will always center around your preferences*. It won't work because you'll be skipping the key step between lack and enough.

Let me remind you about my first two books. In the first, you read how clarity isn't the opposite of confusion. Instead, clarity is a possible result of embracing the true opposite of confusion, which is space. You need space before you can see. Similarly, in the second book, you read that taking action isn't the opposite of being stuck. Seeing is. Once you see, the *feeling* of stuckness typically evaporates. Oftentimes, you don't even need to do anything about it, as you can now see your way out of the stuck position, and usually, that's enough to relieve the frustration and stuck feelings.

Similarly, abundance and sufficiency aren't the opposite of lack.

If you're feeling a sense of lack, there's a reason for it. It's because you've closed yourself off to the natural riches that are always present, within and around you. Whether you believe it to be true or not, richness is already all around you, just as you needn't believe in gravity for it to be operating at all times. And why don't you have access to the richness all around you? Because you've refused it. You've said no to it. You may not believe it right now, but in time you will if you continue along this path. *You'll come to know that this is how it is*, that your current poverty-mentality (if that's what you have) comes from your refusal to invite the richness that's within you and all around you into your life.

So, the opposite of lack is welcoming in what life has to offer, saying yes to more of life. What was once an empty house becomes richer through your welcoming attitude of hospitality to all that life would bring to you, the good and the bad.

Another way to say this is that we don't end up at lack because we fail at abundance or enoughness. *We end up at lack because we stop welcoming in what is offered (whether we like it or not).*

15 Why not welcome in what's being offered?

Now, why would anyone stop welcoming in what was being offered?

It's because what's being offered isn't always to our *liking*. What's offered today may be a slap in the face, a speeding ticket, or a cutting remark by a friend. Do you still welcome that in, not just with a begrudging attitude but with openness and gratitude? If not, you're rejecting the richness of life, whether on the surface, or in your heart. And in turn, you're missing out on the richness that's being offered.

And why do we reject such richness?

It's because many of us live a life based upon preferences or likings. ***We allow in what we like and keep out what we don't.*** **That, in essence, is the root of lack.** It's what starts the cycle of not enough, as we're basically keeping out whatever portion of life it is that we happen not to like. If we dislike and push away 50% of what life seemingly has to offer, then we're keeping out 50% of the richness available to us. If we dislike and avoid 98%, then we're keeping out 98% of that same richness. It's as simple as that.

If you want to learn to get over your sense of lack, you'll need to learn to loosen your attachment to your preferences, as much as you are able.

It's natural to like and dislike things. We're biologically built to have preferences. For example, we've evolved to dislike the smell of poo as well as rotten flesh.

It's one thing to have these preferences. It's another to be attached to them.

For example, I like certain kinds of music and not others. But if I get so attached to what I like, and I'm in a car and someone turns on music I don't like, and I become upset or discontented by what I'm hearing, it shows a strong attachment to my likes and dislikes. It shows a closed-mindedness to new information. It shows a kind of pride in musical taste. It's more or less the same cluster of mental and emotional states as described in the earlier chapters of this book.

In 12-step programs there's a saying, "Principles before personalities." It refers to the importance of abiding by principles such as honesty, open-mindedness, willingness, humility, tolerance, kindness, compassion and so on, rather than responding to people's personalities, which are simply a matter of our personal *preferences*. The saying points to a way of living that allows us to overcome personal attachments and make wiser choices in the long-run, governed not by our own likes and dislikes but by long-standing principles. It points to a way of living that can lead to greater harmony with others as well as within our own lives, which some would consider an integral aspect of true abundance.

16 A poem like a mantra

The beautiful poem below by Rumi (translated by Coleman Barks)[2] should be the guide for all who would seek true abundance in their lives.

The Guest House

This being human is a guest house.
Every morning a new arrival.

A joy, a depression, a meanness,
some momentary awareness comes
As an unexpected visitor.

Welcome and entertain them all!
Even if they're a crowd of sorrows,
who violently sweep your house
empty of its furniture,
still treat each guest honorably.

---

[2] Reprinted here with permission from Coleman Barks.

He may be clearing you out
for some new delight.

The dark thought, the shame, the malice,
meet them at the door laughing,
and invite them in.

Be grateful for whoever comes,
because each has been sent
as a guide from beyond.

17 Equanimity

So what is this quality of mind that allows us to live with greater freedom from attachment to our personal preferences?

It's called equanimity.

It can also go by the names of serenity or acceptance. But I use equanimity partly because of its etymological richness, and partly because of how multifaceted it can be in comparison to the other terms.

If you happen to lack equanimity or acceptance in your life, you might consider sitting with and eating your lack, as the nutrient found within it is equanimity itself. In other words, *you'll find yourself drawn toward embracing an equanimous state of mind as you process and digest the feelings of lack within you.* Stated in its logically-equivalent contrapositive, if you fail to eat your feelings of lack and simply do your best to avoid and/or overcome them, then you'll be far from equanimity and peace with things as they are.

The rest of this book will focus on what equanimity is, how it can be cultivated and how it leads us toward a feeling of enough and even plenty.

Let's start by considering the dictionary definition of equanimity: mental calmness, composure, and evenness of temper, especially in a difficult situation.

Note the idea of dealing with a difficult situation. It's similar to how most speak of acceptance, as in "I'm trying to practice acceptance of the situation." In fact, people rarely use the word acceptance when they're having a pleasant time. For example, no one wins a million dollars and says, "I had to practice acceptance at my good fortune." We might hear instead, "Once I won the million dollars, I began to see who my true friends were, which was extremely eye-opening and even upsetting for me. That was something I had to come to accept."

Both equanimity and acceptance point toward this idea of finding some semblance of peace in the midst of difficulty.

When we look at the etymology of equanimity, it comes from the Latin *aequus* + *animus*. Aequus means "impartial, even, or flat." And *animus* means "mind or spirit." So equanimity can be thought of as a mind or spirit that is (1) impartial, (2) even, and/or (3) flat.

We'll address each, starting with the first.

18 Equanimity as an impartial mind

I want to recount an old Taoist story that I think captures well this quality of an impartial mind.

Once upon a time, there was a farmer who had many beautiful stallions. The village people would say of the farmer, how lucky he was to have such beautiful horses.

The farmer would just say, "Maybe, maybe not."

One day, the horses all ran away, and the village people said, "How unfortunate it is for the farmer to have lost all of his horses."

The farmer simply replied, "Maybe, maybe not."

A few weeks later, his horses came back, trailing with them many other beautiful, wild horses. Upon seeing this, the village people remarked at how fortunate the farmer was now to have so many more beautiful horses.

The farmer simply responded, "Maybe, maybe not."

One day, the farmer's son was training the wild horses and was thrown off violently, causing him to break both of his legs. The village people heard of this and said, "What a great tragedy to befall the farmer's son."

The farmer simply nodded, "Maybe, maybe not."

A few weeks later, all able-bodied young men in the village were forced to go into battle. Most of them died. But the farmer's son was spared because he was not able to walk. The village people remarked at how fortunate the farmer was to still have his son alive.

The farmer simply said, "Maybe, maybe not."

The farmer in this story embodies an impartial or equanimous mind—that is, a mind able to see the good and the bad within a situation and hold them both concurrently. The farmer is non-reactive to each of the dramatic situations that arise, as he is able to maintain some peace about himself through these episodes. There's a sense of ease in how he goes about living.[3]

---

[3] There's also something interesting going on in terms of narrative structure. Notice how it doesn't follow any traditional narrative form, like what is found in just about all conventional

Contrast this with how many of us might react to unpleasant news or to an unwanted situation. For example, imagine that something precious is stolen from us. Many of us would lean emotionally and attitudinally toward the negative and see mostly the bad of the situation, and based upon this negative view, we might adopt a darker attitude toward life or to others, making us paranoid or less trusting. Through this darkened view, we might slowly make our lives smaller. Maybe we build a tall wall around our property, or lock down everything we own. Maybe we begin cutting out people from our lives whom we suspect of shady motives. And yet, maybe it's one of those people that might have introduced us to the opportunity of a lifetime a year from now? But we won't know that since we've chosen to shut them out of our lives, and in parallel, shuttered ourselves into a smaller life.

We simply don't have any idea what we're losing when we choose to stop welcoming in what life offers us. This doesn't mean that we mail out open invitations to robbers and thieves. What it does mean

---

movies or novels. The story simply continues without end. There is no real end, no climax, no heroic journey, no moment of personal insight or redemption, and so on. *The protagonist rests in an open state of not knowing.* One might even interpret this unusual narrative "non-structure" as indicative of the reality woven around an equanimous mind, that it is a series of external events, each perhaps seen as blessed or tragic from the outside, and yet, seen as simply another life event from within, where the true "event" taking place is in the mind that's able to remain unmoved, at peace, and open to possibilities and opportunities.

is that if life brings a thief into our lives, we might notice that whatever was taken from us was no longer needed, and in turn, allows more space in our lives for something more fitting to our current needs. It means that we can uphold an equanimous attitude that's impartial to outcome. The stronger and deeper this capacity for equanimity, the more likely we'll detach from what we want and learn to see the richness that still surrounds us. We'll more likely loosen our fixation upon rainwater while standing in a clear, beautiful and bountiful river.

19 An exercise to help cultivate an impartial mind

When we think of equanimity, we might think of it as feeling peaceful and easy. So we might think that if we want to be peaceful, the path to it must also be peaceful, even easeful? I think this is possible, but I also think that the goal and the path can feel very different, that to get to a place of equanimity can take mental and emotional effort, as in work. It may not necessarily feel peaceful *and easy*. Instead, it may feel more arduous, or more specifically, like creative or imaginative work that can sometimes take tremendous mental and emotional effort.

For example, if we were to win a million dollars, many of us would see mostly the good in that moment, if not *only* the good. But can we imagine being gifted a million dollars and seeing ten things that would make it a blessing and ten things that would make it a curse, and hold them both in mind? It takes a certain agility of mind to do this, but it's something that can be cultivated in us. The process of cultivation may feel like work, but once this habit of mind is established within us, then the product of that effort can lead to a greater sense of peace and acceptance.

The question then becomes, *how can we begin to cultivate a mind that is able to see both sides of a situation, especially in the midst of difficulties?*

Below, I'll introduce an exercise that when practiced regularly will develop an agility and fluidity of mind that can move one past the usual emotional constraints. In other words, this exercise can help us to develop a mind that thinks beyond what our emotions incline us toward. Because many of us tend to have a harder time seeing the good in the seemingly negative, I'll focus the exercise in that particular direction. The other direction is simply the practice of prudence and caution, which evolutionary psychology suggests is a more natural capacity in us, so we'll let evolution do its job there!

Exercise

Try thinking of a situation in your life that causes some *mild* upset or frustration for you. *Nothing too heavy such as depression or rage-filled anger,* but more along the lines of a situation or circumstance that you might say "sucks."

Here's an example. A few years ago, I drove to Los Angeles (in Southern California) from Northern California on Thanksgiving weekend, and as would be expected, there was heavy traffic. A seven-hour drive became closer to eleven-plus hours. By the ninth hour I was thinking, "This traffic sucks!" I wasn't angry at anyone. I was mostly frustrated. I felt very tired.

So here's the exercise:

1. First, form the sentence in your mind, "Such and such situation sucks." For example, "This traffic sucks."
2. Rate the degree of "suckiness" on a scale of 1 to 10, with 1 being not sucky at all and 10 being very sucky. I would have rated my situation a 9.
3. Take the original sentence, and change the "sucks" into "is great" or "is wonderful," as in "This traffic is wonderful."
4. Ask yourself how much you believe this new thought, on a scale of 1to 10, with 1 being no belief whatsoever to 10 being deep, genuine belief. In my case, I didn't believe the traffic was great at the time, and so it would have been a 1. *Of course this traffic isn't great. It's bullshit*, is what I was thinking. And yet, I was still able to mentally form the opposite sentence of "this traffic is great" because one

doesn't have to believe a sentence that one mentally forms and recites.

So you have two numbers. The original number *will* be higher than the new number. *So this is not an impartial mind.* It would be nice if they were the same, whether both 5's or both 1's. It's unlikely that both will be 9's, as the original charge will drop with the exercise.

5. Now write down or think of reasons that make the new sentence true. *You don't have to believe them, but they just have to be true.* It may be challenging for you to come up with genuine reasons that make your "sucky" situation wonderful, but this is where your creativity of mind matters. It's how you're learning to develop a mind that can think past the usual emotional barriers.

Try the exercise right now. Give yourself about 5 to 7 minutes. Try coming up with at least five, if not ten reasons that would make the new statement true.

If you engage honestly in this exercise, in time you might become convinced, just as I have, that the inability to consider a circumstance/event/situation which initially "sucks" and become equanimous about it, is mostly a failure of imagination. It's not an emotional failure or something we're born with or not. It's rooted in the inability or unwillingness to think things through imaginatively enough to see the possibilities inherent within a situation that we're so emotionally against.

When I engaged my mind like this in traffic, I had been on the road for nine plus hours and I was tired, not just from the drive but because I had slept poorly in freezing temperatures in a tent the night before.

So at that moment, I said to myself, "This traffic is great" (which I didn't believe in the slightest) and I started thinking of reasons that would make the new statement true (not whether I *felt* it was true). My first thought was, *if I'm driving at less than five miles an hour, there's very little chance that I'm going to die because if I was going 75 mph in the dark, I could kill myself in an instant, but at 5 mph, I'm probably not going to die right now. So that's one reason why this traffic is so great!* (Perhaps you can sense an undertone of sarcasm?)

It felt silly because some part of me knew that the likelihood of crashing at 75 mph wasn't particularly high for me that night, but my rationale was still true, which is that my chances of death were significantly reduced going less than five miles per hour.

Another thought I had was, *if there's this much traf-fic, it means that the road is being used a lot, and that means that for all the people who put together the highway, their work is being fulfilled.*

And another: *it also means that a lot of people are heading home, where they're likely going to find comfort, and so this traffic is an indication of many homecomings.*

And I continued, *what if I was going at 75 mph, and I got home, and someone shot me? But now because I'm going to be arriving four to five hours later, I might miss being shot to death.*

These are the kinds of reasons I conjured. They may sound far-fetched, but at least they supported the statement that the traffic could be a wonderful thing. I tried mentally reciting every possible thing that could make the current situation "great" even though it went against what I wanted, all while stuck in traffic! And this is the key point. *Whether a situation agrees with our desires or not, doesn't determine whether it's wonderful or great. True liberation is not freedom to do or to get what we want. It's freedom from self, from our egoistic agendas, from our continual wants and desires.* It's not that we stop desiring, but our happiness and peace become independent of whether those desires are fulfilled or not.

Within a few minutes of engaging in this way, it became clear to me that the thought, "This traffic sucks," didn't feel as emotionally charged anymore. Instead, it seemed more like, "It kind of sucks, but it kind of doesn't." *Maybe, maybe not*, became my attitude. I had discharged much of my frustration and irritation around the traffic and the long drive, and now I was driving with a more equanimous mind. I wasn't jumping for joy at the traffic and being a Pollyanna about it. I was simply impartial and emotionally unperturbed by the situation.

There's one reason above all the others that I haven't yet mentioned that made the traffic wonderful for me. In fact, it's the same reason that makes any "sucky" situation wonderful. It's that I want a mind that's at peace. I usually want this more than anything, and if reality *is* (as it is), and I'm fighting reality, then I can't have peace. In other words, when I'm in traffic and my mind says that the traffic sucks (which is just a different way of saying, "This traffic shouldn't be"), then I have a mind that's counter to and contrary to reality as it is. I'm fighting things as they are with my mind. There's little chance for peace then. On the other hand, if there's traffic around me, and I think that the traffic is wonderful (which is simply another way of saying, "I approve of this traffic existing here"), and I have even the slightest belief in that, I'm that much closer to peace, because I'm closer to being in alignment with things as they are. That is, my thinking and my attitude are in sync with reality, and thus, not fighting it.

And so that was the main reason why I wanted for there to be traffic, simply because there was traffic then. If there's traffic, I want there to be traffic. If there's no traffic, then I want there to be no traffic. If someone doesn't like me, I want them to not like me. If they like me, I want them to like me. *I want my mind to want what is.* I want for my mind to want things as they are because this is the quickest path to peace. It doesn't mean that I resign myself to things just as they are without any effort at improvement. Not at all. If I want to improve things, I can generally do a much better job at it with a peaceful and equanimous mind. Establishing this sense of peace and acceptance comes first. Then I can see the situation more clearly, and I'll likely avail myself to greater and more impactful possibilities rather than pushing my own agenda in the situation borne of my frustrations, irritations and lack of equanimity.

Just to note, this is different from *denying* my feelings of frustration. I *knew* that I was frustrated, but I also knew that my attitude of, "This traffic sucks," was exacerbating the frustration. As I used my mind to come up with reasons in support of the opposite attitude, the emotional charge behind the attitude of "this traffic sucks" dissipated, not to the point of being in denial of the reality of traffic being there, but to the point where I genuinely felt impartial about the situation.

When you look at your own list from this exercise, did the emotional charge of the original statement drop off a bit? Has your attitude evened, as in, "Maybe this is good, maybe this is not so good?" Do you see where this is going? We're trying to be like the farmer in our story.

I've found that the exercise doesn't work so as well when I'm in the throes of deeply disturbing emotions.[4] But with a situation that's at the level of "suckiness" (which for me is where I find 99% of all unpleasant experiences to be, especially if I'm living mindfully so that very little goes beyond that), this exercise allows for a fairly innocuous way of maneuvering one's way to a sense of evenness or impartiality of mind, that is, to equanimity. I say "maneuver" because the exercise is more a mental exercise of maneuvering—as opposed to an emotional one of processing. In fact, I find that I rarely believe the new thought (i.e., "Such and such is great") in the beginning. As such, it's mostly an intellectual exercise at first, but eventually, something shifts underneath. It's similar to making a gratitude list, which oftentimes starts out as a mental exercise, but pretty soon, feelings of gratitude begin welling up.

---

[4] I would obviously suggest professional help with depression and deeply disturbing emotions, or else, establishing a robust meditation practice within which one might practice specific techniques of transforming highly-charged emotions, only under the supervision of a qualified teacher, of course. For those interested in learning to build a daily meditation practice, you might consider my book on the topic, *Contemplative Meditation: How to Build a Sustainable Daily Practice*, which will be released sometime in late 2017.

What if you're stuck on the original thought of how crappy the situation is? What's originally called for in this exercise is more mental or creative energy rather than emotional, and yet, sometimes we can get stuck on the thought of "Such and such really sucks." If you find yourself in a situation like that, one way to loosen one's attachment to such a thought is to check in with the body.

Suppose you're in traffic and the thought is, "This traffic sucks," and you find yourself entrenched in your belief around this. What you can do is check in with how your body is doing when you think that. You'll likely be tense. But what happens when you think, "This traffic is great," *when you're in traffic*? Most likely your body relaxes. You might even notice yourself smile or even laugh at the ridiculousness of the thought. *So it becomes easier to take the side that relaxes as opposed to the side that keeps you tense* (since both thoughts are simply opinions). Just noticing how your body reacts differently to the opposing thoughts allows you just enough mental breathing space to begin with the exercise. And from there, you can commence with the exercise.

As a side-note, this same approach of utilizing our bodily reactions to our thoughts can be helpful when we're lying in bed unable to sleep. We can notice which thoughts cause tension and which ones relax us. Then we can ally ourselves with the thoughts that relax us. You might even begin to catalogue which kinds of thoughts cause tension in your body and which kinds release tension. You might find some interesting correlations.

To return to the exercise, *the goal here isn't to convince ourselves that traffic is great while we're in traffic.* There would be unnecessary strain in that. And it's also not an impartial attitude. Instead, the goal is to use this exercise to loosen our attachment to the belief that it's bad, that it sucks. It's to arrive at a "maybe, maybe not" quality of mind. It's to arrive closer to equanimity. The goal is not to get our "it's great" belief level to a 10. It's more about lowering our belief and attachment in the "it sucks" down from a 10. We're not trying to *solidify* something positive, which in itself can be cause for further tension. Instead, we're trying to *loosen* the resistance we may be holding toward reality as it presents itself.

Try this exercise with a few different situations and see if the mental effort doesn't lead you to a more balanced state of mind and feeling. The more you work with this particular mental muscle, the stronger it will become, and in time it won't be hard for you to hold, very naturally and without much effort, both the good and bad of a situation with impartiality, that is, with equanimity.

20 Hard gratitude

That last exercise may have reminded you of another more common one—that of creating a gratitude list. But rather than just a simple gratitude list, one could call it a "hard gratitude" list. It's a term I learned in passing from Claudia Azula Altucher and James Altucher in their book, *Become an Idea Machine: Because Ideas are the Currency of the 21st Century.*

For those of you unfamiliar with the practice of gratitude lists, it's simply jotting down a list of things that one is grateful for. It's common to sit down with a notepad and list anywhere from one to ten things, as a daily practice. What makes the hard gratitude list interesting is that we don't just list the easy items such as, "I'm grateful for my health; I'm grateful for, my friends; I'm grateful for my home" and so on.

Instead, we focus on an area of life that's not working out to our liking. Maybe we're in a job we dislike and think it's the worst job in the world. So we become grateful for the job. We write, "I am grateful for this job *because…"* Or maybe we're single yet deep inside, we desire a relationship. So we become grateful for being single. We write, "I am grateful for being single *because…"* and we list ten reasons. Or maybe we're sick with diarrhea and nausea. So we find reasons to be grateful for our malaise. "I'm grateful for this illness *because* this diarrhea is obviously cleansing my system better than a juice fast ever could. I'm grateful for this illness *because* it's the only way I'll slow down and give myself some rest. I'm grateful for this illness *because* I tend to be more open to new information when I'm suffering and lying in bed like this all day."

It's the "because" or reason, that's important. That's the training of our mind, looking for reasons that would make the *seeming* curse into a blessing.

It's the same basic idea as the exercise in the last section. What the hard gratitude list gives us is a practice for developing greater equanimity, of learning to become more impartial and detached to our wants and preferences. We learn to see the gifts in the *personally* undesirable aspects of our lives and ourselves.

When we're able to appreciate those parts of our lives that are the most difficult to love and appreciate, how much easier it becomes to love and appreciate our lives as a whole. In other words, we're able to embrace and welcome in life more wholly, and in turn, our lives become fuller, not just externally, but in our hearts as well.

The practice of hard gratitude lists helps us to draw closer to a truth of life, captured in the story about the Swiss psychotherapist Carl Jung, who would greet seemingly good news from friends with consolation, and seemingly bad news from friends with congratulatory cheers. He understood that life had a way of balancing itself, that what appeared to be "good" news on the surface sometimes contained within it a hardship, and "bad" news usually came with hidden blessings.

By practicing a hard gratitude list on a regular basis, we can begin to see the more evolutionarily challenging side of what Jung practiced, seeing the good in the seemingly bad. (We're already predisposed to see the bad in the seemingly good, which is a good thing for the survival of our species. It's also a good thing in that most of us don't need to train ourselves in that direction.)

21 A personal example of practicing hard gratitude

About a year ago, I received a call in the early evening from my mother letting me know that my father had been diagnosed with lymphoma in the eyes. The doctors had found a tumor in both eyes that they believed was causing his deteriorating vision. In fact, he was already blind in one eye, and gradually losing vision in the other.

I took in the news as I do with just about any information, mostly as facts, then I noted a wave of thoughts and emotions, primarily of worry and fear. Then I got busy with my evening and eventually went to bed.

I awoke the next morning with a sharp pain in my upper-left tooth. It was so painful that I made an emergency appointment with my dentist who told me

I had ground my teeth so hard in the night with (subconscious) worry that I had cracked one of my molars, and that it needed to be pulled out immediately! I was thinking, *What?! That seems a bit extreme!* But in the end, that's what was done. I wasn't pleased with this turn of events, but what was done was done. What was more worrisome for me was that I feared that I'd do the same thing with another tooth, and so not knowing what else to do, I sat down to write a hard gratitude list on my father's cancer.

Having done gratitude lists for a long enough time, I wasn't particularly daunted by the task. I began it without much fanfare. Just pulled out a notebook and started a list.

Here are a few that came to mind almost immediately.

1. I would likely have an excuse to take more trips down to see my parents (about a seven to eight hour drive).
2. My father might be more open with me emotionally.
3. I might find myself becoming more open and vulnerable with him as well.
4. If he got through it, maybe he'd come away from the experience with some newfound understandings that would make for a better quality of life afterwards?

5. Maybe I could be of some use, which would be a blessing in itself.
6. I would likely learn a bit more about myself in the process.

As I continued building this list, I noticed how my heart gradually felt more open, and how I relaxed around what was happening. Although I would never tell my father about the list (as it seemed a bit insensitive to be telling him how grateful I was for his cancer, in the midst of his suffering), I kept adding to it without pause until I felt genuinely grateful at the turn of events, and it was an attitude and feeling that felt firmly established in me.

One or two weeks later when I visited my parents at a time when they had scheduled a number of doctor visits (for which they showed a noticeable degree of anxiety and worry), I spent a good deal of time with them while also accompanying them to the appointments and helping them communicate with the doctors. In addition, my father needed a new computer system to accommodate his failing eyesight, and as the "technologically-inclined" son, I helped them put together a new system.

During the visit I found it easy to focus on *their* welfare. While I could feel a palpable sense of fear and anxiety in their being, I felt myself carrying little of it within myself. So I could "take it in" from them, and process it with them. In other words, I could be there for them.

I'm confident that had I not done the hard gratitude list prior to my visit, I would have brought my own fears and anxieties, my own agenda and an over-focus on my own hardships in this process upon them, and in the process, unnecessarily burdened them through a difficult period for them. But as it was, I felt myself a support for them, and in fact, they expressed what seemed to me to be heartfelt appreciation for this support later.

Becoming grateful for a difficult situation doesn't mean that we become Pollyannas who pretend things are okay when they aren't. Instead, it means that we establish an attitude of acceptance and openness to whatever it is that's occurring, and through that, we're able to be more present to ourselves as well as to others. Being present to others in this way is a form of emotional giving or generosity; and recall, the root of emotional richness and safety is emotional generosity. If we want to experience life as being emotionally abundant and safe, we provide this for others. Establishing a robust sense of gratitude in our minds and hearts allows and supports that capacity in us.

22 Gratitude as a path

Gratitude seems to be all the rage nowadays. Lots of people are talking about its value and benefit to our well-being. I think it's great also.

What it does is that it helps us to develop a more equanimous mind. It keeps us looking at things in a more *open* capacity, *allowing in* what life has to offer. And through receiving what life offers, we grow richer, *not in some narrow and preference-based (i.e., ego-based) manner, but in a way that life itself nurtures and provides.* And out of this larger sense of richness, we have something of value to offer others. And finally, in offering to others, we grow even fuller or richer in some manner of being. Remember that generosity begets wealth, whether it be of a material, emotional, or spiritual nature.

This is the path.

On the other hand, gratitude isn't some magical, wishful force that brings about abundance for no reason. Gratitude works because it opens us up to what is. It opens us up to both the "good" and the "bad" that life serves up. We stop closing off from the "bad." Gratitude becomes the mental muscle that allows us to stay open to all that life serves us. Through this process we grow, and we gather unto ourselves the goodness as well as the difficulties that cause us to deepen. This deepening furthers our gifts. And without such deepening, what we offer won't have as meaningful or profound a value for others. Instead, it'll more likely be flimsy and lightweight fluff, not so hard-won with depth. So in this spirit, we receive the difficulties and challenges of life with a grateful heart, knowing that it will lead to greater and deeper offerings from ourselves to others.

(Imagine that you got only what you wanted, and you could avoid all the hardships in life. You would have something different to offer others. But how genuine is that? How real is that for the rest of us who suffer disappointment, disillusionment, loss, grief, devastation, and so on?)

In short, because we welcome in what we like as well as what we don't like, we have something of meaning and value to offer others. And when we begin to offer these things to those around us, the world reciprocates in its own manner.

Like I emphasized earlier, gratitude isn't a magical, wishful, affirmation-based trick. You can make a gratitude list till you're blue in the face, but if you're also holding onto the idea of life working out according to *your* likes and dislikes, you'll be missing the point. It won't lead to anything magical or wondrous. You'll just sound like a Pollyanna who sees only the positive side of things, and yet, you'll still be *self*-centered (a "self" constructed out of your preferences) and feeling the same "not enough" feeling of lack. So instead, *allow gratitude to soften your grasping at your preferences.* Allow it to open your heart so that it can welcome in all that life has to offer. Take it all in. With gratitude.

23 Confidence

What happens next—when we soften in our grasping toward our preferences, and begin allowing what we don't prefer into our lives, as well as releasing our attachment to what we do prefer?

We actually begin to experience greater *trust* in the natural flow of our experience.

This trust is what often shows itself as genuine confidence. Or stated inversely, true confidence is undergirded by a deep sense of trust. When we examine the etymology of confidence, we find *com* ("with") + *fidere* ("to trust"), and we can hear intimations of the deeper meaning of the word, which is that to have confidence with living is *to have trust with* the process of living. (Further, to have confidence in ourselves is to have trust in ourselves.)

This kind of confidence is independent of accomplishments and possessions. It's not based upon how much money one makes, how many friends one has, how admired one is by others, and so on. Rather, it's based upon a direct relationship with life itself. It's what some refer to as an inner confidence, but I find this expression a misnomer. It's not *inner*, but a *relational* confidence—a trust of one's relationship to life itself.

And it's precisely this kind of confidence that allows one to pursue loftier goals, take greater risks in life, live one's dreams, and so on. That is, when we welcome into our hearts, equally, the so-called "negative" experiences as we would the "positive" ones, we develop a confidence in our capacity to move more fluidly with life, and in turn, we open and avail ourselves to life's many and unexpected manifestations, including its myriad and abundant gifts.

24 Equanimity as an even mind

We now arrive at the second interpretation of equanimity, likely the most commonly held view of it. It's the idea of having an *even* mind, an *even* temper, a capacity for being *even*-keeled. A synonym might be a balanced mind.

I'd like to contrast this image of an even mind with its opposite, which would be an *uneven* or imbalanced mind. An interesting thing to consider is where such imbalance might come from.

If one examines the etymology of balance, one finds that it derives from the Latin *bis* ("twice") + *lanx* ("plate, dish, or pan"), as in "having *two* pans (on a scale)." So what causes imbalance? One answer might be, it's in having only *one* pan (on the scale). *That is, it's in being one-sided!*

And usually, that one-sidedness is on the side of ourselves, our preferences, or our habitual tendencies.

That is, our regular egoistic agenda that sides continually with self produces imbalance, and in turn, can cause a loss of equanimity.

In Japanese, there's a word, *katayoru* or *katayotteru*. It means to lean or to be inclined *to a side*, sometimes, even biased or prejudiced. It's this image of a "leaning-(to-one-side)" mind that I'd like to explore as the antithesis of equanimity as an even mind.

25 Eating—no, real eating!

"How you do one thing is how you do everything."

Back in the late 90's, a book titled *Eight Weeks to Optimum Health* by Harvard-trained Dr. Andrew Weil hit the best-seller charts, and I was one of many who read the book. Inspired by the ideas in it, I chose to subscribe to a 52-week newsletter that Dr. Weil published at the time. Each issue consisted of about six to ten pages of the latest vitamin, herbal, exercise, meditation, nutritional information out there.

I found many of the ideas interesting, but within a few weeks, I felt overwhelmed by the sheer volume of information, and so, I stopped reading the newsletters. But because I had paid for them, I was reluctant to throw them away. So they began piling up in the corner of a bookshelf, and each time I'd look in their direction, I'd feel a twinge of guilt that I'd try my best to ignore.

Finally, near the end of my subscription, I picked up the latest issue and began browsing it just so I could assuage my guilt. The article I happened to alight my eyes upon began along the lines of (non-verbatim), "By now, you may be overwhelmed by many of the dietary and supplement-related information I've provided. Allow me to make it simple for you. If there's one principle that should guide you in your dietary choices, it's *variety*. Keeping a varied diet will help you to cover your nutritional needs." Or something along those lines.

What a relief! I thought.

I had studied a bit of evolutionary theory in my doctoral studies, and somehow, this same idea had come up then, that for an ecosystem to be robust and healthy, it required diversity.

So, I took to Dr. Weil's suggestion immediately. But also, I had grown up with parents who both believed that the worst kind of diet was one that was *katayotteru*. In other words, they regularly warned me against eating a diet that leaned in any particular direction. They often suggested that it was important for me to expand my diet, not narrow it. (As a young adult, I actually did the exact opposite in as many ways as I could and naturally suffered the consequences.)

But for many years now, I've tended to eat just about everything (even the occasional cream-based product despite having to take lactase pills!), and I have a fairly robust system. I've come to see health, not as *needing* to eat healthy foods, but one that has a rich variety, and thrives on healthy foods while also not being overly-sensitive to so-called "unhealthy" foods. Everything in moderation, as they say.

I find this to be its own kind of richness.

We can sometimes gain insight into a person's psyche through their relationship to food. Those who eat a narrow band of food oftentimes tend to live their lives along a narrower band that shows up in their choice of friends, activities, and interests. If done in a conscious manner based upon sound principles and with a relaxed attitude, this can lead to a greater sense of health and well-being, but when clung to with a sense of attachment to one's identity, it can point to some element of despair or tightness of mind underneath. And when done out of mere preference—that is, likes and dislikes—it can lead to a severe imbalance in one's diet. Or it can show up in a subtler manner as a sense of psychological unease, of not quite feeling that one is living one's life *fully*, or a nagging sense as if there were something important missing.

And yet, I would suggest that it's the narrowness—the leaning into a particular lane, if you will, *especially when shaped primarily by preference*—that creates the bias, the imbalance. When we begin inclining into foods that we like and away from those we don't, we more easily create a nutritional imbalance. We lose the evenness or balance.

The mind is similar. One way in which we can transfer this idea of a varied diet is that of fostering a mind that is varied in its mental and emotional "diet." We don't just welcome in pleasant thoughts and emotions. We also welcome in unpleasant ones. We don't live our lives clinging to what's pleasant and trying our best to avoid what's unpleasant. (On a relational level, this can show as not clinging to those we like while allowing in those we don't.) We welcome them both in as they would come. In this way, we foster a mind that can remain more even. We learn to serve ourselves on two plates, that of pleasant and unpleasant experiences. (And the fact of the matter is, we don't need to do anything for this to be, as life itself has a way of serving both dishes. It's just in our capacity to welcome in both that allows for our experiential diets to be balanced and whole.)

26 A small practice of sorts

Eating new and unusual foods is one of my favorite parts of travel, next to making new connections and friends.

And yet, a few years ago, I also noticed that I had a tendency to order the same three or four dishes at any given restaurant when I dined out *while in town.*

At the time, I used to frequent a Thai restaurant on at least a weekly basis. I usually ordered one of three dishes. And yet, their menu contained over 30! So I decided to make up a little challenge for myself. I would commit to try every dish on the menu before repeating a dish I had already tried. The idea was that I wouldn't need to travel in order to live with a more adventurous and experimental spirit. I didn't quite make it entirely around the menu as I just couldn't get myself to order the sweet peanut dishes (which I still have trouble accepting as anything other than a dessert), but I did try every other dish besides those.

Even though there were many I didn't enjoy, the experience of trying each dish was a revelation. It was a wonderful exercise in not "leaning" into a particular groove or habitual eating pattern.

I share this as a small practice or discipline that can be consciously engaged in to widen one's palate as well as to becoming more cognizant of one's leanings or biases in food choice, but also, in understanding the mind's tendency to lean into a groove of preference.

27 Another two practices

God, Grant me the serenity to accept the things I cannot change,
The courage to change the things I can,
And the wisdom to know the difference.

The "serenity prayer" above is an equanimity prayer. It fosters an *even* attitude between letting go of that which we have no control over, and attending to those things we do, and it's the wisdom to distinguish between the two that allows us to maintain the needed *balance* for "serenity."

For those of us who have recited this prayer many times, we know its power in restoring us to some semblance of balance and peace.

In Theravada Buddhism, there are also equanimity practices, which consist of reciting and resting into the meaning of particular phrases. One phrase that's meant a lot in my own practice is, "This is how it is," which I originally learned from Kamala Masters, a Western Theravada Buddhist meditation teacher.

Suppose I'm grappling with someone else's suffering. I'll quietly and slowly say to myself, "This is how it is." Somehow, this allows me to come to a place of acceptance. You could try it. Think of something that's troublesome to you, and say those words to yourself, "This is how it is." Maybe you notice how your heart begins to open to the situation. Opens as in "What can I do? I feel sad about it, but this is just how it is." Reciting the phrase isn't a prayer. It's also not a magic spell. It doesn't heal someone else, but it allows us to keep our hearts open, and in turn, be more responsive and less reactive.

Further, "This is how it is," isn't a passive proposition. It doesn't mean that we resign ourselves dejectedly to things as they are. It's more that we're confronting something that's difficult to look at, that we otherwise may not want to embrace as a fact of living, and we're simply looking at it as it is. Maybe for the first time. We're letting it in.

Maybe you're considering the acute suffering of someone close. Deliberately reciting or thinking to oneself, "This is how it is," can allow for the utter pain of this fact to pierce into our hearts and to permeate our being. There can be deep peace and even release in that, and later, when we spend time with this person, we can bring a more open-hearted, accepting, and softened quality in our bearing, which would be in strong contrast to not having allowed in the pain of the situation, likely leading to a compulsion to "fixing" the situation just because we can't stand things as they are.

Or let's say we're profoundly miserable. For most of us when we're unhappy, we don't really want to accept and allow for our misery. We don't want to know it. We're trying to escape from it, fix it, overcome it, or change it. But when we're trying to change something, we're resisting it, which often keeps it in place.

But when we say, "This is how it is," it gives us a pause that allows us to take it in *as it is*, saying this is just how it is right now. And creating that space makes us less reactive toward ourselves, whereas if we're not truly acknowledging and embracing things as they are, we could start acting out in unconscious ways and making decisions that don't serve our best interests.

For myself, when I say, "This is how it is," such as when I'm upset and angry, my heart opens, and it feels as if I can be a little more compassionate with myself for having that anger. And that little bit of compassion can create space within the anger, so the anger doesn't feel so solid. It opens up a little bit. It can dissipate from there. Or I can play with it. Maybe channel the energy for something good. It opens up, and I may think, "Wait, other people are angry. I've triggered anger in others through my actions and behaviors. Maybe I could be a little more mindful of my own actions in turn?" And it all starts with this momentary pause, this space within the anger.

So the next time that you find yourself feeling mentally uneven or imbalanced, try thinking of the situation at hand and reciting, "This is how it is," not in a resigned and defeated manner, but with a gentle and accepting tone. See if that doesn't begin a gradual process of restoring some semblance of inner balance.

28 Equanimity as a flat mind – in relationship

So far, we've explored the notion of equanimity as having an *impartial*, or "maybe, maybe not" mind, as well as having an *even* mind. In this section we'll explore equanimity as having a *flat* mind.

To start this third interpretation of equanimity, we'll begin with a simple exercise inspired by Google's social media platform, Google+, where you're able to designate contacts into different categories. Unlike Facebook where you simply select someone as a friend or not, in Google+ you can categorize the "levels" of the relationship between friends, family, acquaintances, and the like.

Exercise

On a blank sheet of paper, draw four ever-widening concentric circles. Put yourself in the very center (as "self" or "me" or your own name). In the space between the first and second circles—that is, in the first "ring"—put those people you consider to be part of your "inner circle," or those you hold closest. In the next ring, put the rest of your friends, and in the last ring, acquaintances, colleagues, and so on. Outside of the farthest circle will be everyone else.

Take a few minutes to do this now.

The intent of this exercise is to help you see how you hold the people in your life. If you can bring that image to mind right now, you might notice that it looks almost like a topographical map, where each layer can be thought of as belonging to a different altitude, with yourself at the top (or bottom) of this mountain (or crater) of sorts.

One way to practice equanimity is to think of these circles or levels as dissolving—that is, the whole terrain *flattens* out. There's no longer a sense that the people near to you are any more important or worthy of a happy life than those farther away. Certainly you yourself are no longer the center of the circles—the "king of the mountain," if you will—because the circles are now gone. It's now just one big tribe of humanity. If you included dogs, cats, mosquitos and the like, then it's one big tribe of sentient beings. There's no longer an inner circle of close friends, acquaintances, and so on. It's simply all beings. One all-inclusive tribe.

This doesn't mean we should deny our feelings of fondness and care for those with whom we have a long history of relationship. Our feelings just are, and sometimes they can guide our choices for the better (although not always). Rather, this is about how we *intentionally* hold the people and beings in our lives. It's a method for viewing our relationships, so as to allow for choice, divorced of clinging and aversion as much as we are able.

It's one thing to treasure those relationships we've nurtured and attended to across years and decades. It's another to cling to them unwisely or to use them as a way to lazily exclude others from our lives. The intention to hold all beings as equal, not just to one another but to ourselves, allows us to operate from a less self-serving and egocentric perspective, and can open up our relational life in unexpected ways. Without the trappings of pre-conceived links and ties, we're more likely to approach our interactions with others—from long-term relations to brand new encounters—with a freshness of perspective, the kind that can give rise to meeting the other *for who they are in that moment.*

This also doesn't mean we try to diminish our care for those who we feel close to, but instead, we try to treat those we don't feel close to with the same care and attentiveness as we would someone we have loved for years.

This equalizing of beings is the intention that's held in cultivating equanimity as practiced in some schools of Buddhism. Traditionally, it's accomplished not using circles, but instead by directly fostering an attitude of regarding all beings (including ourselves) as equal in importance to one another. *Not one over the other.*

The reason I suggest the use of circles is that oftentimes a contrary or contrasting approach can work more effectively than a direct one. Just as one crouches *down* before leaping *up*, or one can tense a muscle before relaxing it more deeply, seeing the ways in which we hold beings unequally can be the springboard to releasing that view (most likely built around our preferences) into a larger and more impartial one. Another justification for the use of circles is that it can be more effective to *start where we are* rather than attempting to land directly at the goal.

Regardless of the approach, the reality is that those people/animals/beings we put in our inner circle don't actually exist there, nor do the others in their corresponding compartments. They exist simply as they are. They have complete agency and freedom within themselves. They don't exist as we've defined them in our minds. Holding people in these groupings is akin to putting them into boxes. It's a conceptual construct that we place upon others that's temporary, unnecessary, and oftentimes limiting, not just upon others, but also upon our own capacity for love and care.

Through learning to hold all beings on par with one another, we can expand our humanity, and also draw closer to genuine unconditional love (as in love that's not dependent on who or how the recipient is).

Besides thinking of it as dissolving our circles, another way to think of it is as expanding our inner circle so that in time, it encompasses everyone and all beings. And yet, this will be difficult if we remain attached to our hierarchical and subjective arrangement of persons and beings in our lives, and for this reason, we engage in the dissolving and/or flattening of the conceptual map of our relational terrain.

29 Tribal mentality

It's natural to want to create a tribe or circle around which we feel a sense of belonging, as that can have its own richness, but sometimes we can become overly attached to this feeling of belonging, and in turn, lose our larger connection to life itself. Whether it's through religious, political, social affiliations or the like, it's not hard to slip into a tribal mentality with its appeal of belongingness. But when we think in terms of "inner circles" and categories of inclusion, we intrinsically exclude others from such circles. It's this exclusivism that can then lead to increased attachment to those on the "inside" and greater aversion to those "outside" of such circles. Such a view of self and others can make it hard to establish genuine equanimity in our daily dealings with others.

But it can also limit our sense of richness and resourcefulness.

In an article on forbes.com, Michael Simmons suggests, based upon network science, that one of the most important variables in predicting career success is the nature of one's network connections. The graph below summarizes the basic idea, that one's level of performance as measured in accomplishments, evaluations, promotions, and so on, is higher when one exists within "open networks," which means that one interacts *across* a number of clusters of networks. In contrast, in a "closed network" one is embedded within a primary cluster, where everyone knows one another and usually has similar interests and/or worldviews.

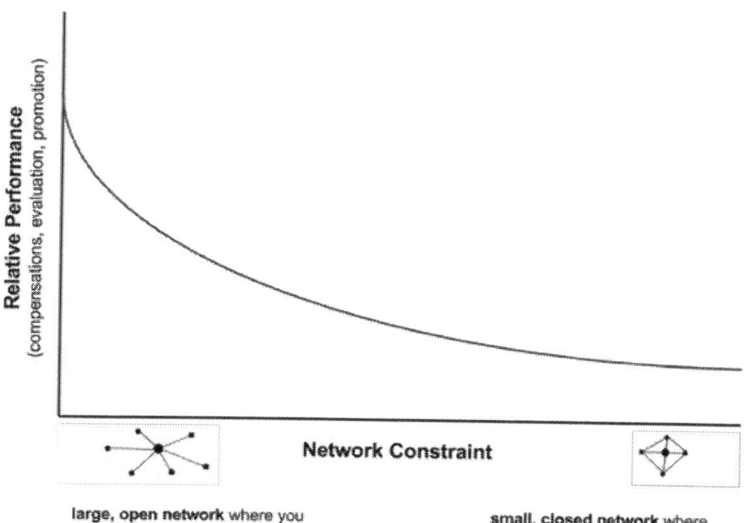

In other words, being able to traverse across different types of groups is a strong predictor—up to 50%, according to the study cited in the article—of work success. Simmons writes that existing within an open network confers certain advantages not available to those who live within a closed network, such as having a more accurate view of the world due to the capacity to triangulate one's views, having more breakthrough ideas due to exposure to atypical combinations of ideas, having value as a translator or interpreter of ideas across different groups, and so on. In short, living in an open network confers a *richness* and *resourcefulness* not available to those living in closed networks.

But if living within an open network is so advantageous, why don't all of us choose to live as such?

As Simmons argues, the natural tendency among a group of people is for the like-minded, with similar interests and goals, to gather together because it's more comfortable to surround oneself with others who confirm our worldviews. So there's a sense of safety in belonging to a closed network of people. In turn, there can be a resistance to networking across different groups as doing so may be taken as betraying our already established ties.

The liability here is that our view remains limited compared to a person who's living in an open network. For the latter, they're gaining a different perspective from each of the groups, so their overarching view might be like looking at the proverbial elephant from multiple perspectives instead of just one. They'll likely have a more complete picture of reality.

Ideally, we want to belong to many different clusters of networks. We want to find a "home" among many different groups of people if we're interested in experiencing a greater sense of richness and resourcefulness in our relationships. But our preference for safety and comfort in seeking out a tribe can get in the way of moving freely among different networks. *It's precisely equanimity as a flat mind that allows us this freedom.* We don't hold the networks or circles so tightly in our minds. We can cherish these groups, but when we begin to create an identity around belonging to one in particular, we've moved from cherishing to enmeshing ourselves into a group.

If one takes seriously the idea of dissolving the lines, the natural conclusion is that there is really only one true tribe, and that is the *tribe of all beings*. It's the ideal tribe because no one is excluded (well, other than non-beings).

30 A very simple practice

The idea of dissolving the various lines that we draw in our minds among the people and beings we know and don't know, is similar to a simple practice I was once given—to consider the person in front of me as being the most important person in my life at that moment.

Although we may have a long history with certain people in our lives (usually referred to as friends and family), if we're talking to a stranger at a store or on a bus, for example, then we can try to bring all the attention and presence to that encounter as if that stranger was the most important person to us in that moment. It's a wonderful practice for being present and available to all, one being at a time, and it's also imbued with a tremendous sense of freedom.

31 Who are we in all of this?

Belonging to all (groups) isn't to say that one should be a chameleon and try to fit into all groups. Living in an open network means that one isn't driven by a need to fit in so much as to learn from and offer benefit to each of the groups that one interacts with. There isn't the pressure to fit in and to belong, and so, there isn't the need to change one's personality much like a chameleon.

When I was younger, I tried very hard to belong to certain groups and to "fit" myself into them, thereby losing something of myself. I would sense an inner struggle when I didn't feel as if I fit in, as if I was doing something wrong, and thus, the subsequent despairing attempts at fitting in. Now this same feeling reminds me that, of course, I'm not going to fit in 100% with any group. There's no need for that to happen. I don't eat spaghetti everyday despite enjoying it a lot. I don't expect that all my nutritional needs are going to be met by spaghetti. Likewise, I don't expect one smaller tribe to meet all of my emotional, mental, spiritual needs. There are other groups where I can connect in a different way. Being able to traverse across different clusters or subcultures of people is part of the richness of relationships I get to enjoy in this life. And it's in the practice of loosening my clinging to notions of an "inner circle" that allows me to make a home with most I encounter.

32 A short piece from a while ago

Forgive me this indulgence, but I want to close this section on the third interpretation of equanimity by sharing a short piece I wrote about ten years ago around this same idea. Although the circumstances of my life have changed since then (as they always do), the conclusion I drew then still holds true for me today.

Homelessness

I have never had the instinct or sentiment for children or family. But I have had, for most of my adult life, a strong pull toward some sense of home. First there is the physical building that I call home. I have filled it with aspects of myself, and somehow it has meaning to me as a place of safety and warmth.

Then there is the person in this life who loves me—and I love also—who happens to live in that same place. Being with her is like being home also. I prefer thinking of my life with her as my home, and less so the physical building, because I am then not locked down by geography. We could be traveling together, and somehow I am still at home anywhere in this world with her.

But there is also the sense of being at home within myself. In particular states of mind, brought on usually by rapt concentration, stillness of heart and mind, the beauty of nature, wholesome company, and so on, I find myself at ease in this world. I feel a lack for nothing. I prefer this home to the singular person and to the building because I'm then bound to neither. I imagine this is somehow related to the vision of freedom that the Buddha and others like him sought in pursuing the "homeless" life.

I once met a Zen teacher who shared with me that he had made a practice of intending home would be wherever he happened to be standing at the moment. This is not all that dissimilar to another attitude I've practiced at times, of intending that the most important relationship to me in all the world be with whoever happened to be in front of me—a practice I found deeply liberating. Both practices might be looked upon as attempts at making a larger home in this world. Contrary to common "spiritual" belief, I imagine that the happiest among us are in fact the ones with the largest homes.

33 A summary of equanimity

The common theme among the three interpretations of equanimity, from impartial mind through even mind to flat mind is this: loosening our attachment to our own biases, preferences, and likes and dislikes is how we begin to open up to the river of blessings we stand in. When we do so, we come to recognize our intrinsic richness. This inherent sense of abundance *is* the experience of enough-ness, a place from which we can extend genuine generosity of heart and spirit to ourselves and to others, actions through which our experience of fullness continues to grow.

It's not a matter of how much money we have, how many friends we can count, how many trips we've taken, how good we feel, and so on. It's in a recognition of all that flows in and out of our lives, and how allowing in what's wanting to come in (as well as allowing out what's wanting to exit) that can help us to become more conscious of what we offer out to

others, and in that recognition, we experience ourselves as part of the ever-abundant flow of life itself.

34 The end: where to begin?

It all begins with opening up to, acknowledging, welcoming in, and eating our feelings of lack. It begins by recognizing that feeling less than, feeling like we have a bottomless hole in our gut, feeling like we're a piece of crap isn't a sign of something intrinsically wrong with us. Instead, it's an important signal that says, *Pay attention here. Don't turn away from this feeling.* (That is, *don't stuff the feeling, but also, don't flee into your mind by ruminating over questions such as, "Why do I feel this way? Where did this feeling come from?") Instead, pay attention to the feeling itself and allow it to be in you. What seems the worst imaginable feeling is only the outer wrapping of an unimaginable gift. Stay with this feeling for as long as you can, and the gift will unwrap itself with richness beyond what you can currently imagine. If you stay at this for long enough, across days, then weeks, and even months and years, you will see your own life transformed, and the most extraordinary richness and fullness will come to be—a sense of abundance that will come to feel ordinary to you, and only when you step out from that seeming ordinariness will you recognize how utterly extraordinary the transformation will have been.*

In turn, you may even come to seek out experiences that cause these feelings of lack to become triggered in you. You may seek out pursuits where you lack natural ability, where you feel inferior, mostly because you know what they can lead to. And in time, you may even come to find it difficult to find such pursuits, not because you will have gotten accomplished at everything—far from it!—but equanimity will have established itself in your mind so robustly that the feelings of lack will serve no purpose for you at that point, for their true purpose was simply in leading you to your mind's natural capacity for upholding an impartial, even, and all-inclusive mind and heart, that which is the true source and wellspring of enoughness, wholeness and abundance in this life.

35 Postscript

So here we are. We're nearing the end of this book (and a little over halfway in the series as well). I hope that the reading journey you've just now taken has begun to effect a shift in the way you stand in relation to any sense of lack you may experience in your being. As with the previous books, I do suggest that you consider re-reading this a number of times so that the ideas go deeper than just an intellectual understanding.

I hope that I've minimally convinced you that feeling less than or not enough isn't something to panic about, or blame yourself or someone else for, but rather, to interpret as an indication that something may in fact be lacking, and that choices made based upon attachment to personal preference may have a large part to do with that state of affairs, and that loosening the attachment, and in turn, learning to welcome in more of what life offers, whether we like it or not, is at the root of true richness, abundance, and resourcefulness.

If you desire a full life, establishing an equanimous mind and grateful heart *is* a necessary foundation. From there, you'll be equipped with a capacity for genuinely welcoming in all that life offers, and through that, you'll come to be overflowing with life itself, which will naturally flow unto others, and that generosity of spirit will return to you many-fold, resulting in a feeling of fullness and richness, which in the end, is tantamount to standing in the river of life and *knowing* that you are and have been this entire time. [Smile]

The Gifts that Lie Hidden within Difficult Emotions (Part 3): Feeling Lack and Not Enough

Disclaimer: The information provided herein is for educational and informational purposes only and solely as a self-help tool for your own use. Always seek the advice of your own Medical Provider and/or Mental Health Provider regarding any questions or concerns you have about your specific health or any medications, herbs or supplements you are currently taking and before implementing any recommendations or suggestions from any outside source. Do not disregard medical advice or delay seeking medical advice if necessary. This book is not intended as a substitute for the medical advice of physicians. Do not start or stop taking any medications without speaking to your own Medical Provider or Mental Health Provider. If you have or suspect that you have a medical or mental health problem, contact your own Medical Provider or Mental Health Provider promptly. Although the author and publisher have made every effort to ensure that the information in this book was correct at press time, the author and publisher do not assume and hereby disclaim any liability to any party for any loss, damage, or disruption caused by errors or omissions, whether such errors or omissions result from negligence, accident, or any other cause.

About Yuichi Handa

Here is a new picture. It was taken in Yogyakarta, Indonesia in the summer of 2017.

Printed in Great Britain
by Amazon